BOOK OF
BONES

10 Record-Breaking Animals

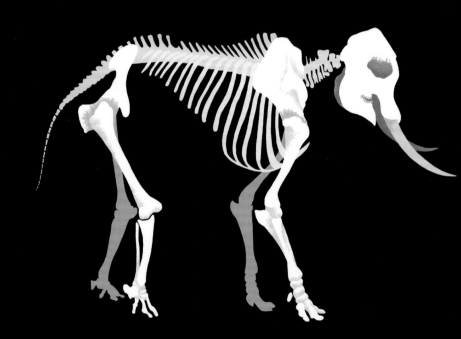

by Gabrielle Balkan
illustrated by Sam Brewster

To my dad, Robin, the first scientist I ever knew - GSB

To the Brewster family for their ongoing support,
and for all the kids who keep asking "why?" - SB

Thanks to all who helped with our bone-related queries, including Allyson Coleman,
Animal Curator at Leesburg Animal Park in Virginia; Anthony Friscia, Ph.D., Professor
of Integrative Biology & Physiology at the University of California, Los Angeles;
the library staff at the Natural History Museum, London; and especially Lee Post,
aka "Boneman," an animal bone enthusiast of epic proportions of Homer, Alaska.

Phaidon Press Inc.
65 Bleecker Street
New York, NY 10012

phaidon.com

First published 2017
© 2017 Phaidon Press Limited
Text copyright © Gabrielle Balkan
Illustration copyright © Sam Brewster

Artwork created with ink on paper and digital coloring
Typeset in Raisonné Demibold and Value Serif.

ISBN 978 0 7148 7512 5 (US edition)
001-0717

Designed by Meagan Bennett

Printed in China

TABLE OF CONTENTS

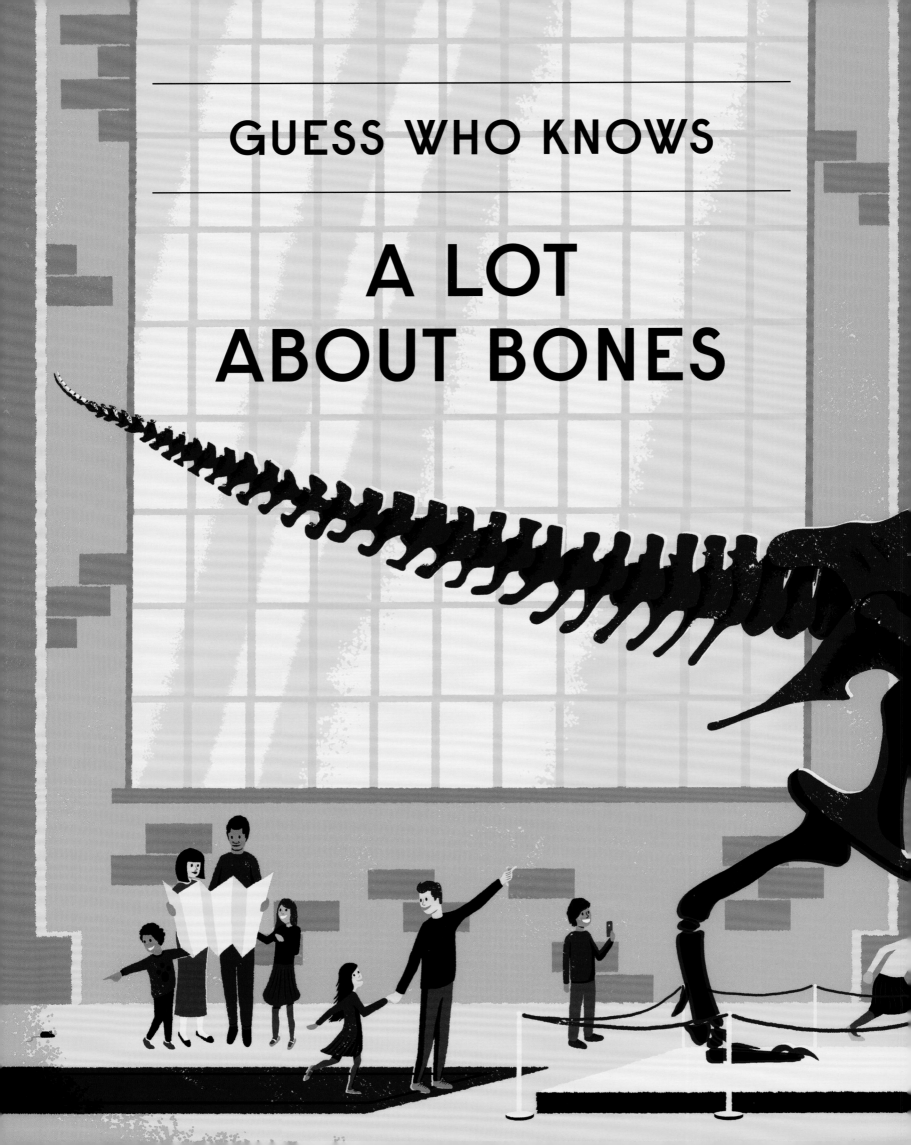

YOU do! You know that the soft part of your belly is not a bone but that the hard part of your rib is. You know that your bones make up your skeleton and that your skeleton gives you your shape. You know that bones come in all shapes and sizes and that most animals—from the tiny mouse to the enormous *Tyrannosaurus rex*—have (or had!) bones inside them!

But do you know which animal has the biggest bone in the world? Or the smallest? Or the spikiest?

You will—as soon as you meet the ten incredible animals in this book. Examine their skeletons and read the clues to guess which impressive animal goes with which special bones. Are you ready?

GUESS WHO HAS

THE BIGGEST BONE

Huge. Gigantic. Tremendous: That's ME. Inside my massive body, I have the world's biggest bone. My mandible, the long bone in my lower jaw, is a whopping 20 feet long. That means three motorcycles could sit in a row on my jaw bone. You have a mandible, too, but yours is small enough to fit in the palm of your hand.

- I live in the ocean.
- I swim great distances.
- I can live for 100 years.

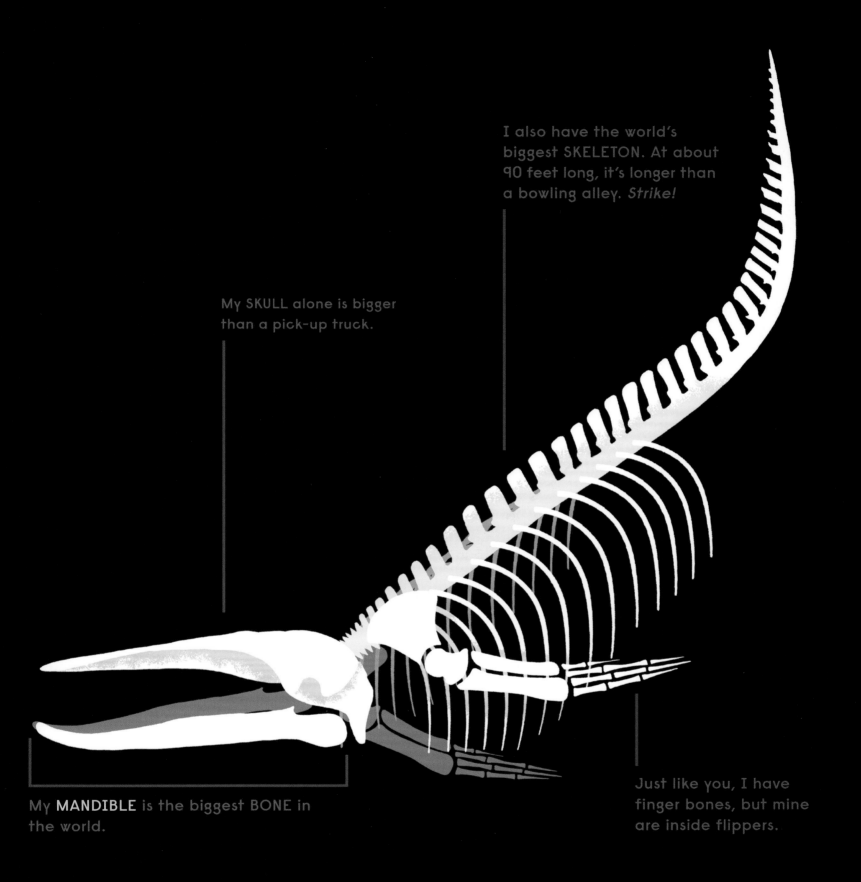

I also have the world's biggest SKELETON. At about 90 feet long, it's longer than a bowling alley. *Strike!*

My SKULL alone is bigger than a pick-up truck.

My **MANDIBLE** is the biggest BONE in the world.

Just like you, I have finger bones, but mine are inside flippers.

Who am I?

I AM A
BLUE WHALE

I'm the world's largest animal. I'm bigger than any dinosaur that ever lived. Thanks to my enormous mandible, my mouth is so large that I could fit one hundred of your friends on my tongue. But don't worry, I don't eat humans, I eat krill: tiny shrimplike creatures that live in the sea. I need LOTS of krill to keep me going. My mandible helps me swallow over seven hundred THOUSAND krill in just ONE gulp! Good thing because I need to eat about forty million krill a day—that's like eating twenty-four *thousand* bath tubs full of jellybean-sized fish!

GUESS WHO HAS

THE SMALLEST BONES

I am teeny tiny. My skull is smaller than your pinky nail. Inside my skull are my ears, and inside my ears are the smallest bones in the world: my hammer, anvil, and stirrup bones. You have these bones, too! Yours are about as long as an eyelash. Mine are about the size of this dot right here: •

— I'm easily startled—and *very* shy.

— I scurry through farmlands, gardens, and olive groves.

— I have a venomous bite.

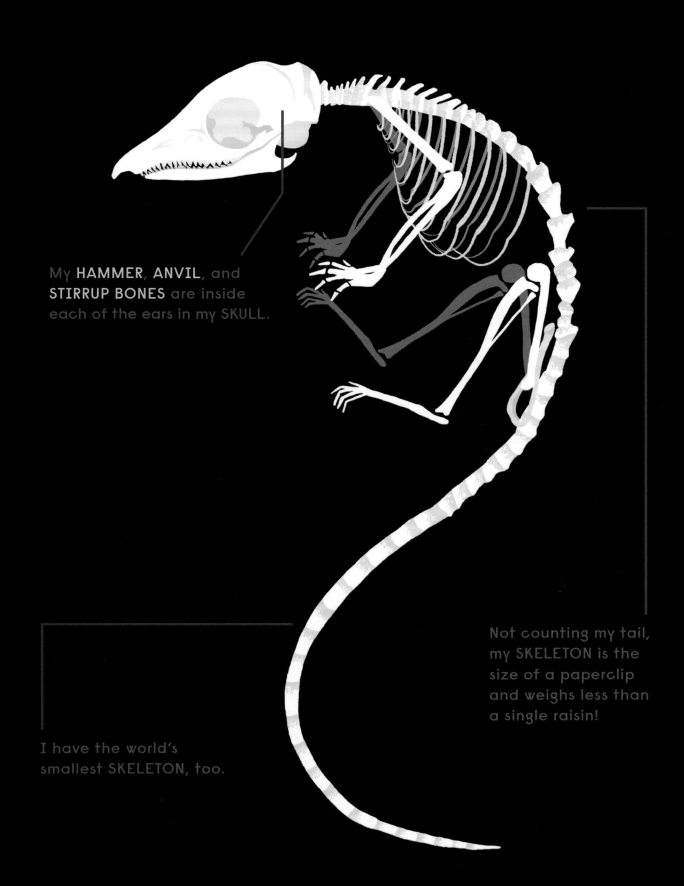

My **HAMMER**, **ANVIL**, and **STIRRUP BONES** are inside each of the ears in my SKULL.

Not counting my tail, my SKELETON is the size of a paperclip and weighs less than a single raisin!

I have the world's smallest SKELETON, too.

Who am I?

I AM AN ETRUSCAN SHREW

I am the world's smallest mammal! I am small enough to bathe in a soup spoon. Both *your* tiny ear bones and *my* tiny ear bones have a giant job: they vibrate to help us hear. *We are* lucky; not all animals have vibrating ear bones. Snakes, frogs, and birds do not. They can hear, of course, but they can't hear everything that I can. *My* hearing is very sensitive and absolutely superb. Good thing, because my eyesight is *terrible*. My ear bones help me hear and find grasshoppers to eat . . . and help me hide from owls, who want to eat me!

GUESS WHO HAS

THE MOST BONES

You are born with 300 bones in your body. I am born with more than one THOUSAND in mine! Most of my bones run up and down my long spine. Touch the center of your back; Can you feel those hard knobs? Each knob is a bone called a vertebra. You have 33 vertebrae; I have around 400! In both of us, our vertebrae add up to make our bendy spines.

- I squeeze rats with my long body before I eat them, head first.

- I have scaly skin and lay eggs.

- I slither through the rainforests of Southeast Asia.

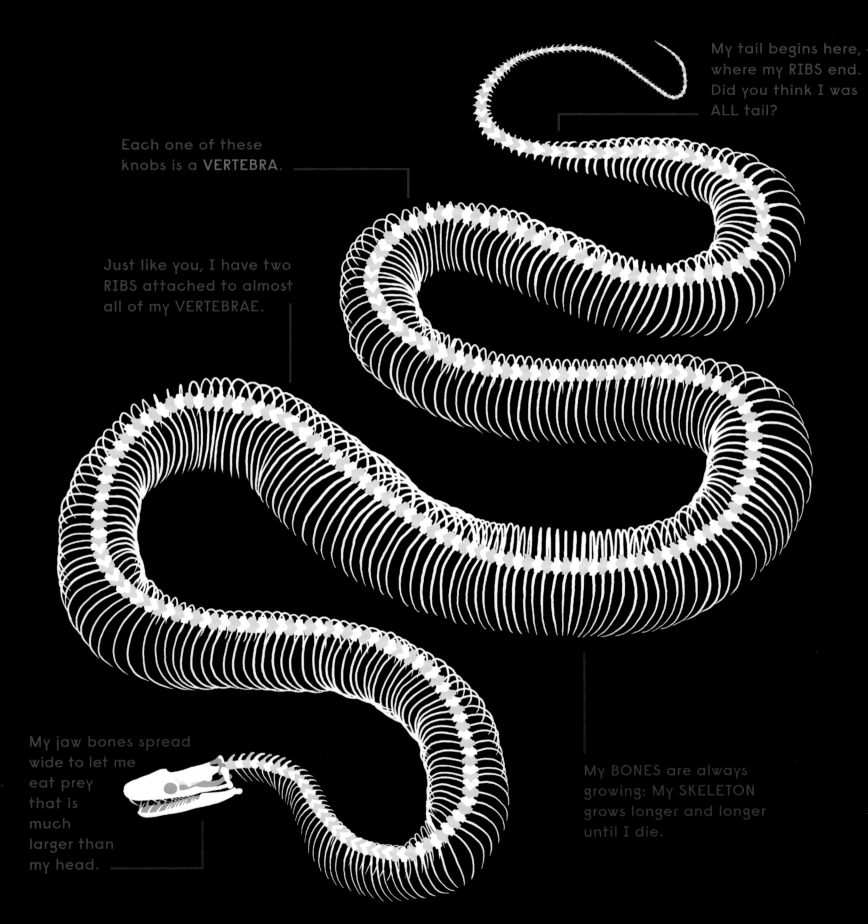

My tail begins here, where my RIBS end. Did you think I was ALL tail?

Each one of these knobs is a **VERTEBRA**.

Just like you, I have two RIBS attached to almost all of my **VERTEBRAE**.

My jaw bones spread wide to let me eat prey that is much larger than my head.

My **BONES** are always growing: My **SKELETON** grows longer and longer until I die.

Who am I?

I AM A RETICULATED PYTHON

Hisssssssss: I am the longest snake in the world! I can grow up to 25 feet long—that's as long as 39 boxes of cereal sitting side by side. To stretch out for a nap, I would need a row of five king-sized beds. The 400 bones in my spine make me very, very flexible. I can wind around trees. I could even wind around YOU. Your spine makes you flexible, too. You can reach high and bend low to touch your toes. I don't even have toes. No legs either, so I wiggle the bones in my long spine to get from one place to another.

GUESS WHO HAS

THE LONGEST NECK BONE

Hello, down there! I didn't see you at first. After all I have the longest neck bone of any land animal. My long neck and leg bones make me tall enough to peek into a second-story window! Just like you, I have seven vertebrae in my neck. But each one of mine is much, much longer than each one of yours. If you stack these vertebrae, one on top of the other, they make a six-foot-long neck!

- I usually sleep standing up.

- I saunter through the grassy plains of Africa.

- I use my long tongue to clean my ears.

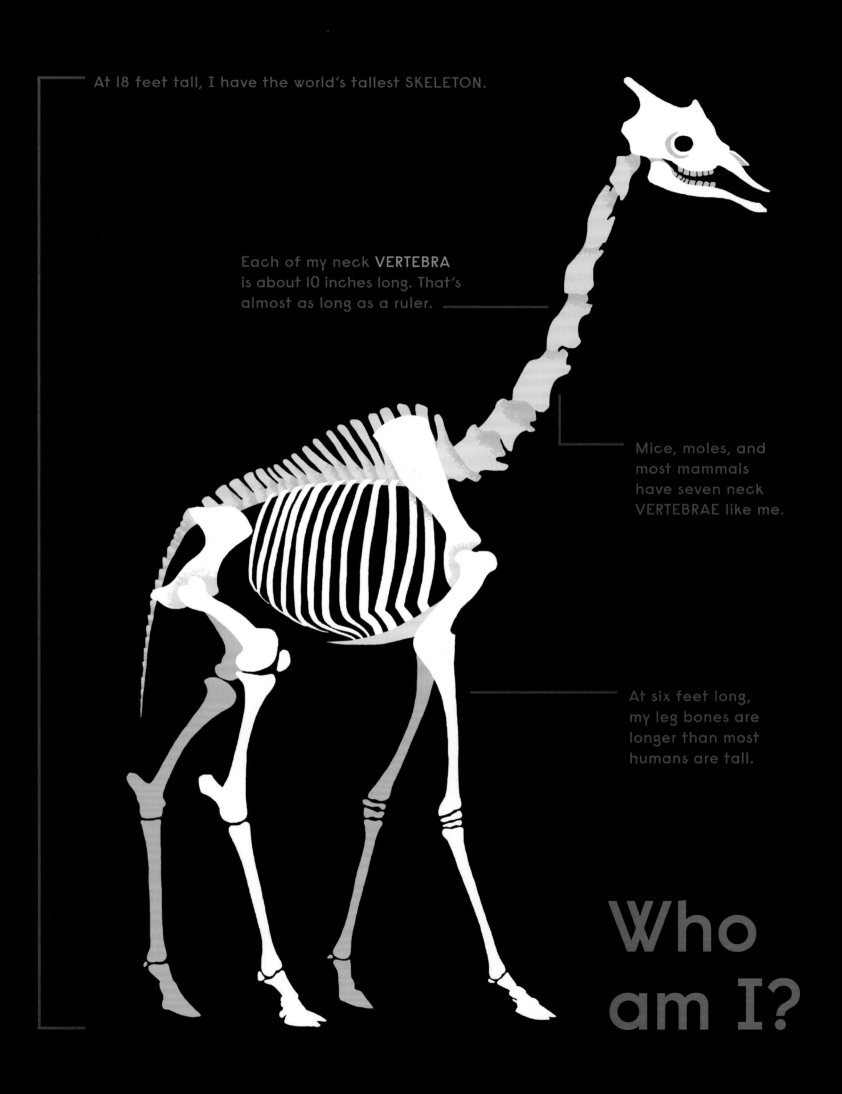

At 18 feet tall, I have the world's tallest SKELETON.

Each of my neck **VERTEBRA** is about 10 inches long. That's almost as long as a ruler.

Mice, moles, and most mammals have seven neck **VERTEBRAE** like me.

At six feet long, my leg bones are longer than most humans are tall.

Who am I?

I AM A RETICULATED GIRAFFE

I am the world's tallest animal. My long neck lets me reach leaves at the very top of tall trees that other animals can't. It also helps me keep an eye out for predators who want to eat me, like the lion. From 18 feet high, I can see far across the open plains of Africa. No lion is going to sneak up on me. And if they do come near, my legs are so long I can kick those lions before they get too close. *Hi-yah!*

GUESS WHO HAS

THE HEAVIEST BONE

The heaviest bone on land is inside the heaviest animal on land. Who's that? That's me! Which bone is that? It's my humerus! You have a humerus, too. It's the long bone in your upper arm that runs from your shoulder to your elbow. My humerus is taller than a dining room table and can weigh 53 pounds—that's as much as a bucket of bowling balls, and maybe even you!

- I roam Africa in giant herds.

- I am the biggest animal on land.

- I flap my giant ears to keep cool.

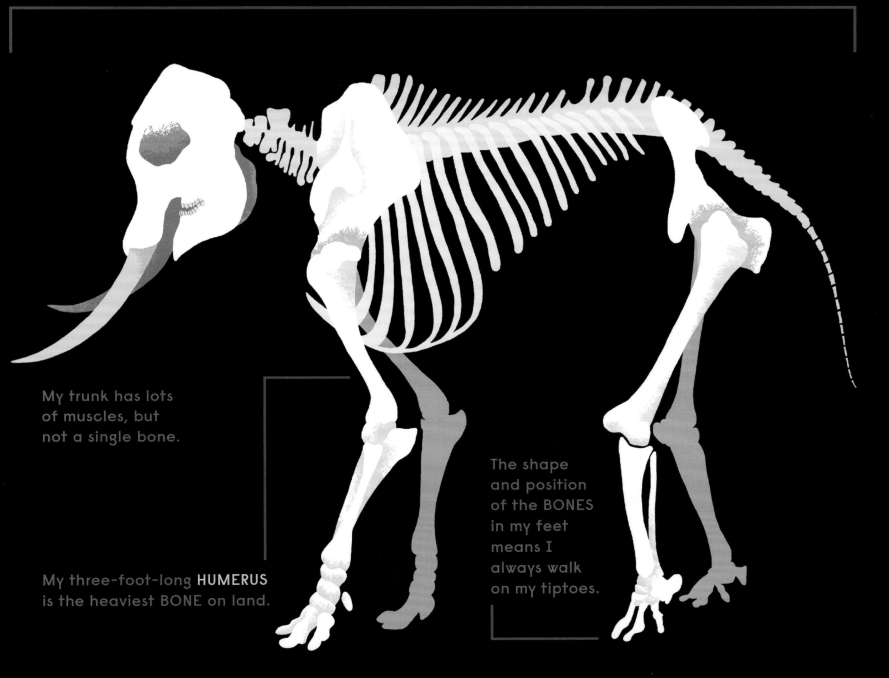

I also have the biggest and heaviest SKELETON on land.
It weighs around 2,250 pounds, more than 10 refrigerators.

My trunk has lots
of muscles, but
not a single bone.

My three-foot-long **HUMERUS**
is the heaviest BONE on land.

The shape
and position
of the BONES
in my feet
means I
always walk
on my tiptoes.

Who am I?

I AM AN
AFRICAN BUSH
ELEPHANT

I am the largest animal on land. My body can weigh up to 14,000 pounds—that's heavier than a helicopter, two forklifts, or four taxi cabs. To carry this heavy body of mine, my legs need to be extra strong. Extra strong bones means extra heavy bones. Just like you and other mammals, the food I eat helps me grow strong bones. In my case, that food is 600 pounds of grass and tree bark a day!

GUESS WHO HAS

THE LIGHTEST BONES

My bones are so light that they weigh less than my feathers! My light bones help me jump, take off, soar, dive, and land—all important skills for a life in the sky. My bones are light because, unlike you and most mammals, who have bones filled with bone marrow, mine are filled with holes, and these holes are filled with air.

— When I dive through the air, I am the fastest animal in the world.

— I prey on other birds and bats.

— I build nests on mountain cliffs and skyscraper ledges.

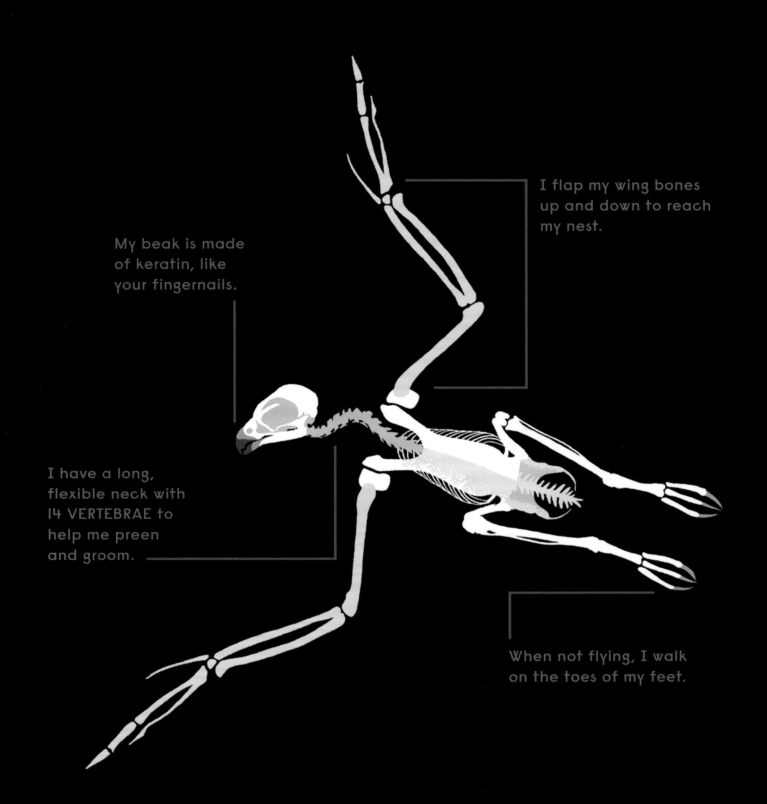

I flap my wing bones
up and down to reach
my nest.

My beak is made
of keratin, like
your fingernails.

I have a long,
flexible neck with
14 VERTEBRAE to
help me preen
and groom.

When not flying, I walk
on the toes of my feet.

Who am I?

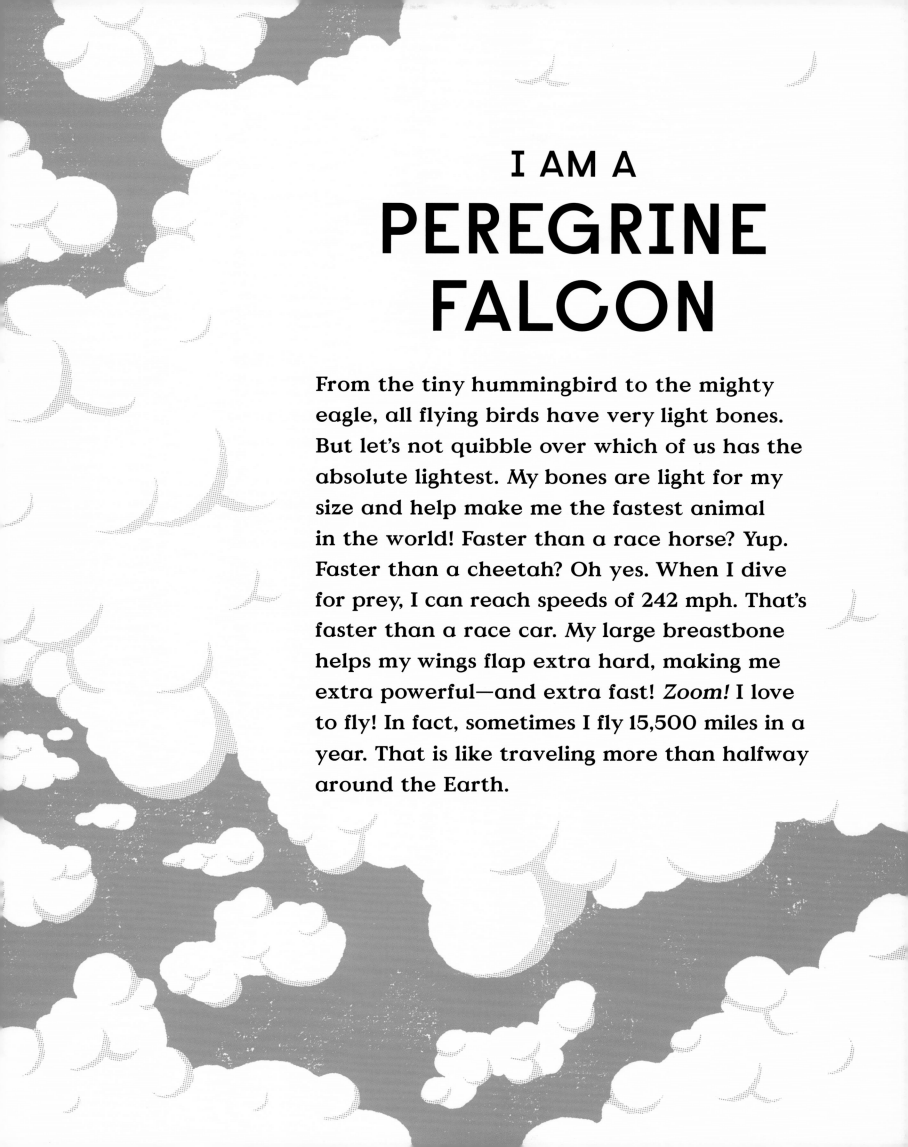

I AM A
PEREGRINE FALCON

From the tiny hummingbird to the mighty eagle, all flying birds have very light bones. But let's not quibble over which of us has the absolute lightest. My bones are light for my size and help make me the fastest animal in the world! Faster than a race horse? Yup. Faster than a cheetah? Oh yes. When I dive for prey, I can reach speeds of 242 mph. That's faster than a race car. My large breastbone helps my wings flap extra hard, making me extra powerful—and extra fast! *Zoom!* I love to fly! In fact, sometimes I fly 15,500 miles in a year. That is like traveling more than halfway around the Earth.

GUESS WHO HAS

THE THINNEST BONE

My phalanges—my upper finger bones—are thinner than a single strand of spaghetti. I have four fingers and a thumb, just like you. But MY finger bones are almost as long as my entire body! They act like kite poles to support the thin skin of my wings. My slender and flexible finger bones help me fly wherever and however I want to, which is usually at night.

- I sleep upside down, snuggled with my family.

- I flit through cool limestone caves.

- I am an amazing flyer...but can't walk very well.

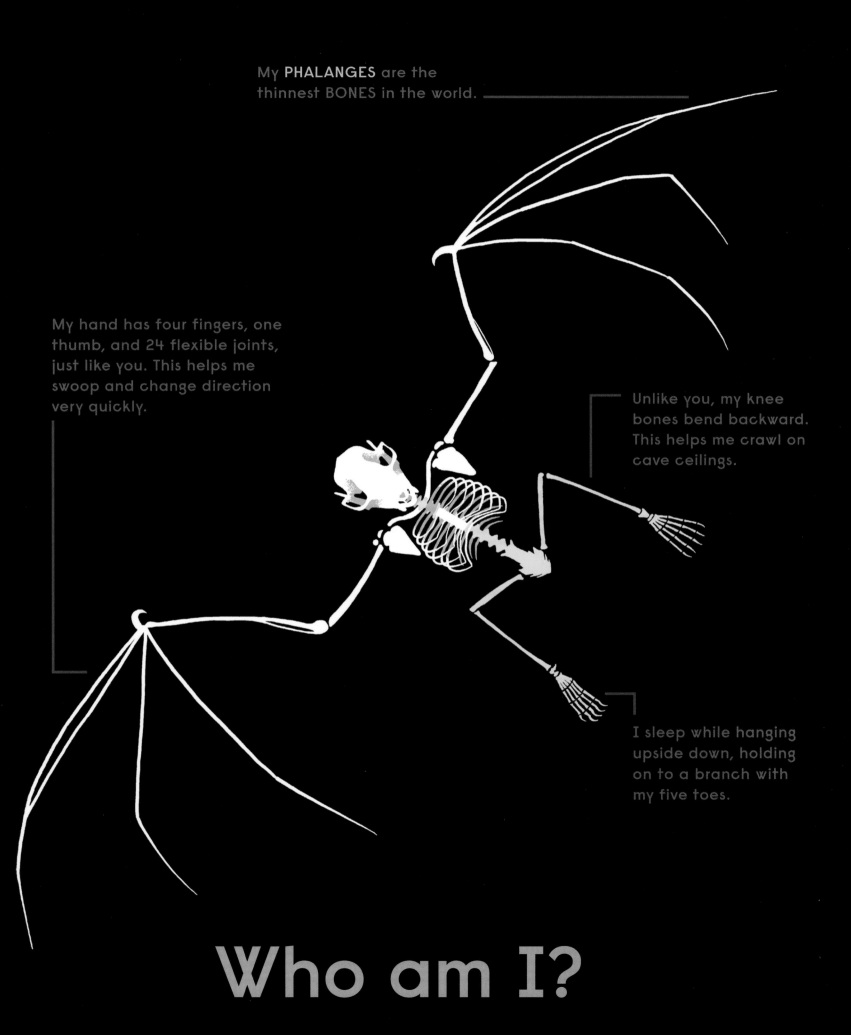

My **PHALANGES** are the thinnest BONES in the world.

My hand has four fingers, one thumb, and 24 flexible joints, just like you. This helps me swoop and change direction very quickly.

Unlike you, my knee bones bend backward. This helps me crawl on cave ceilings.

I sleep while hanging upside down, holding on to a branch with my five toes.

Who am I?

I AM A
BUMBLEBEE BAT

I am the smallest bat in the world. I am so small, I'm named after an insect of a similar size. Guess which one! If your finger bones were as long and thin as mine, your pinky would be as thin as a strand of hair and keep going past your toes! We bats use our wings to fly just like you use your hands to swim. I bend my finger joints to cup the air and push it behind me. This lets me zip through the sky to get to my dinner before it can get away. My dinner is usually bugs. Lots and lots of bugs.

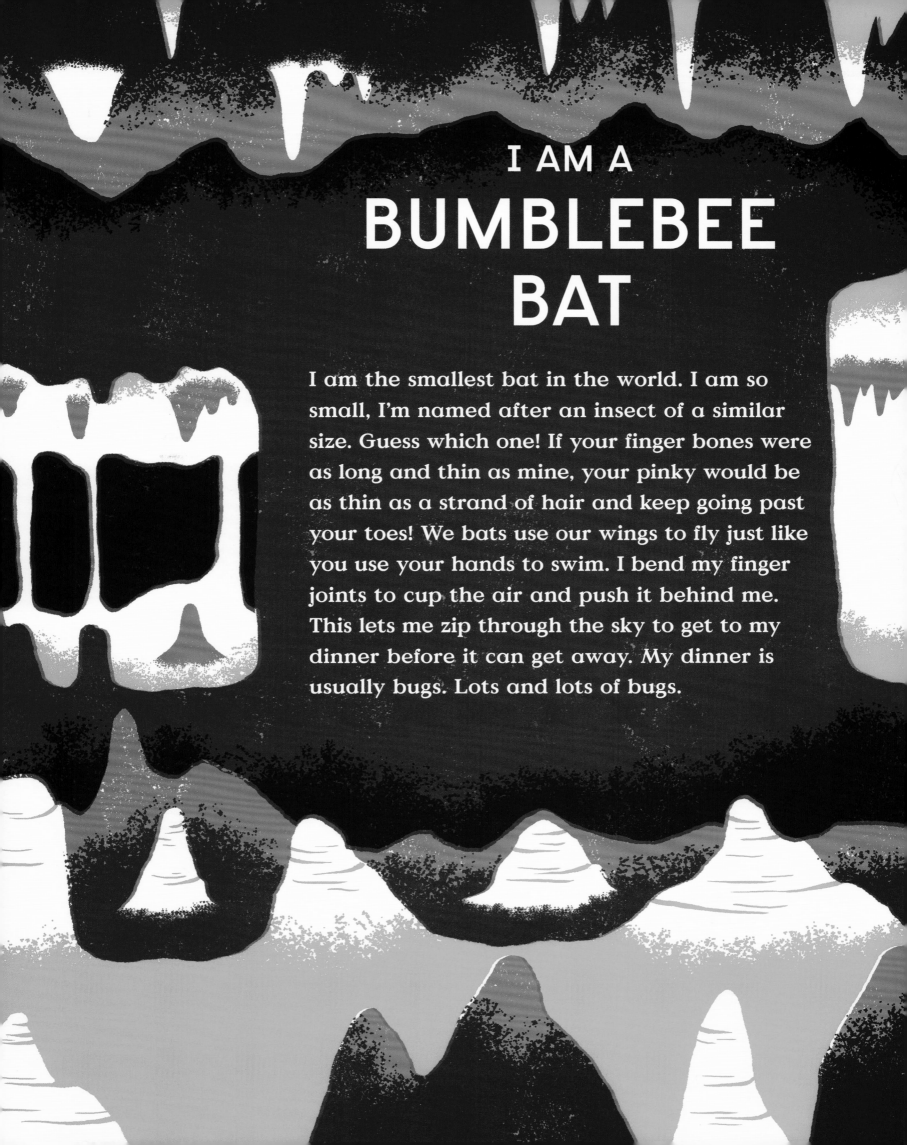

GUESS WHO HAS

THE FASTEST-GROWING BONE

Howdy! Are you checking out my antlers? Get this: they are six feet wide...that's wider than a grand piano! They make for a *grand* entrance. Get it? My antlers are made of bone. It's the same kind of bone that makes up my (and your) skull, but these bones grow on the *outside* of my body. Know what else is surprising? They grow an inch a day! You probably grow one inch in *six months*.

- I use my antlers and hooves to defend myself.

- I live among the spruce trees in the forests of chilly Alaska.

- I usually live alone.

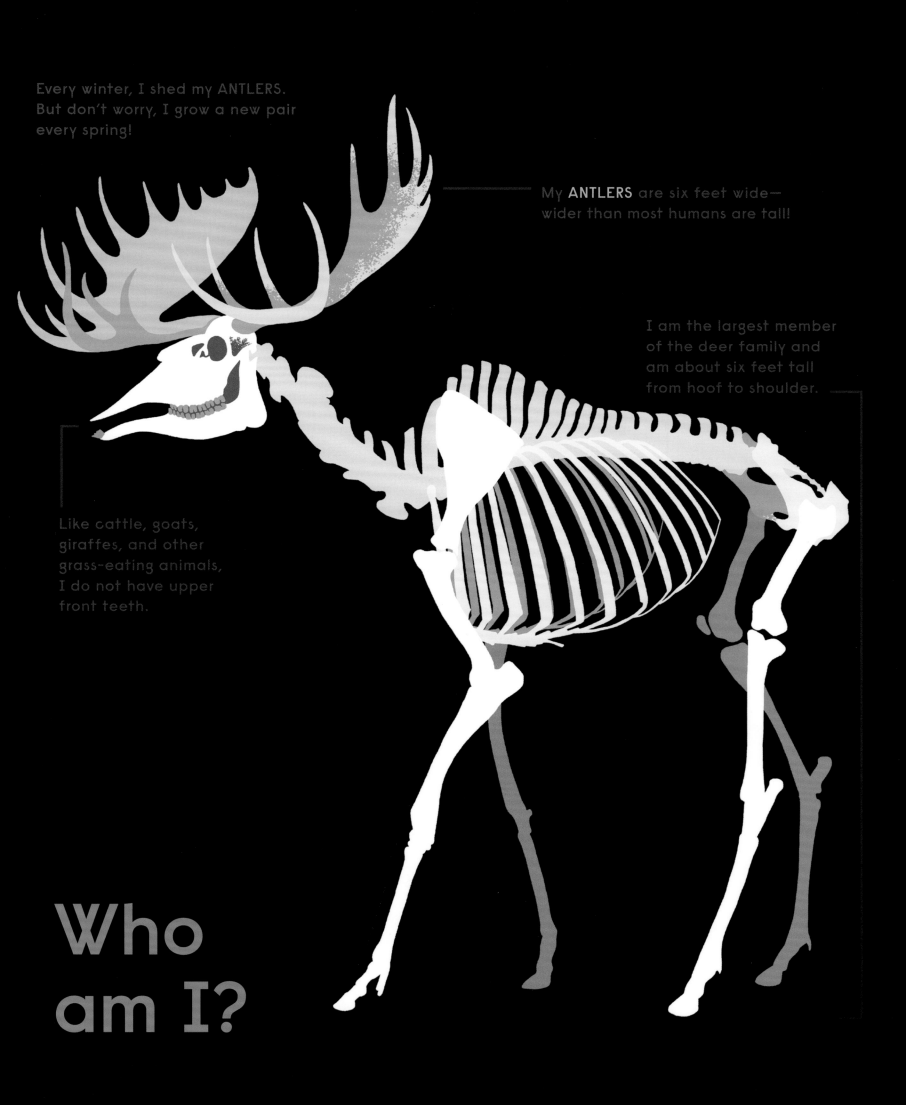

Every winter, I shed my ANTLERS. But don't worry, I grow a new pair every spring!

My **ANTLERS** are six feet wide— wider than most humans are tall!

I am the largest member of the deer family and am about six feet tall from hoof to shoulder.

Like cattle, goats, giraffes, and other grass-eating animals, I do not have upper front teeth.

Who am I?

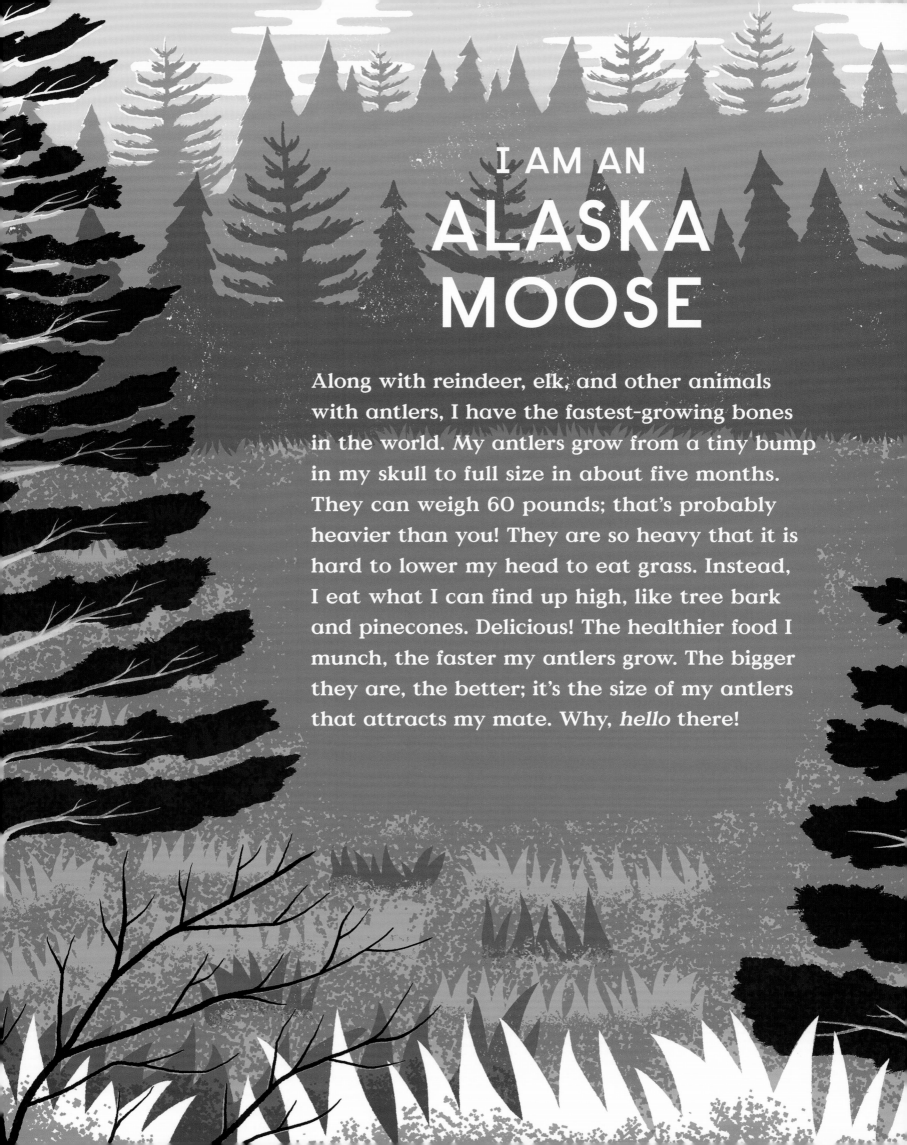

I AM AN ALASKA MOOSE

Along with reindeer, elk, and other animals with antlers, I have the fastest-growing bones in the world. My antlers grow from a tiny bump in my skull to full size in about five months. They can weigh 60 pounds; that's probably heavier than you! They are so heavy that it is hard to lower my head to eat grass. Instead, I eat what I can find up high, like tree bark and pinecones. Delicious! The healthier food I munch, the faster my antlers grow. The bigger they are, the better; it's the size of my antlers that attracts my mate. Why, *hello* there!

GUESS WHO HAS

THE SPIKIEST BONE

Take a look at the spiky bones at the top of my head. These horns grow out of my skull and protect my brain. Smart, huh? I gotta be smart because I'm pretty small and not very fast. It'd be easy for a snake or coyote to catch me. But once they get a feel of my spiky skull they'll drop me. It's sharp! This crown of horns is my best security system.

- I eat ants. Lots and lots of ants.

- I like hot, dry, sandy spots in the Arizona desert.

- I can shoot blood from my eyes.

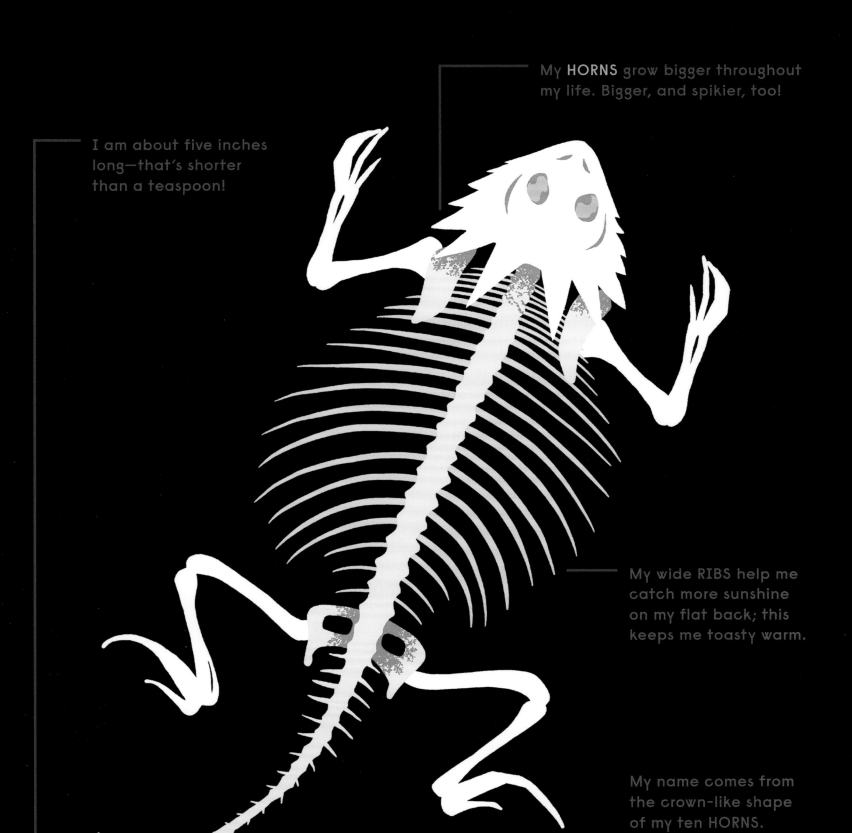

My **HORNS** grow bigger throughout my life. Bigger, and spikier, too!

I am about five inches long—that's shorter than a teaspoon!

My wide RIBS help me catch more sunshine on my flat back; this keeps me toasty warm.

My name comes from the crown-like shape of my ten HORNS.

Who am I?

I AM A
REGAL HORNED LIZARD

I am the only type of lizard with horns that go right around my head, like a queen's crown. My horns are made of bone on the inside and covered with keratin on the outside, which is what your fingernails and a falcon's beak are made of. When a coyote tries to eat me, I bob and nod my head. Seeing my horns move will remind her of how painful I am to swallow. And if that won't keep her away, I can shoot stinky blood from my eyes—who would want to get close to that?!

GUESS WHO HAS

THE FEWEST BONES

Here's a riddle: *Who has a skeleton but no bones?* Answer: *Me.* Instead of bones like yours, my skeleton is made of cartilage, a type of soft, flexible tissue. Cartilage is stiffer than muscle, but not as hard as bone. You have cartilage, too. You can feel it when you touch the tip of your nose. My cartilage lets me twist and make sharp turns when I hunt for prey, preferably stingray—*chomp!*

- I dart through coral reefs in the tropical oceans.

- I grow new teeth throughout my life.

- I'm named after the shape of my skull.

I am usually about 10 feet long...but can grow to over 20 feet long; that's almost as long as an ambulance.

My skull, jaw, and spine are the strongest parts of my body—to help me hunt!

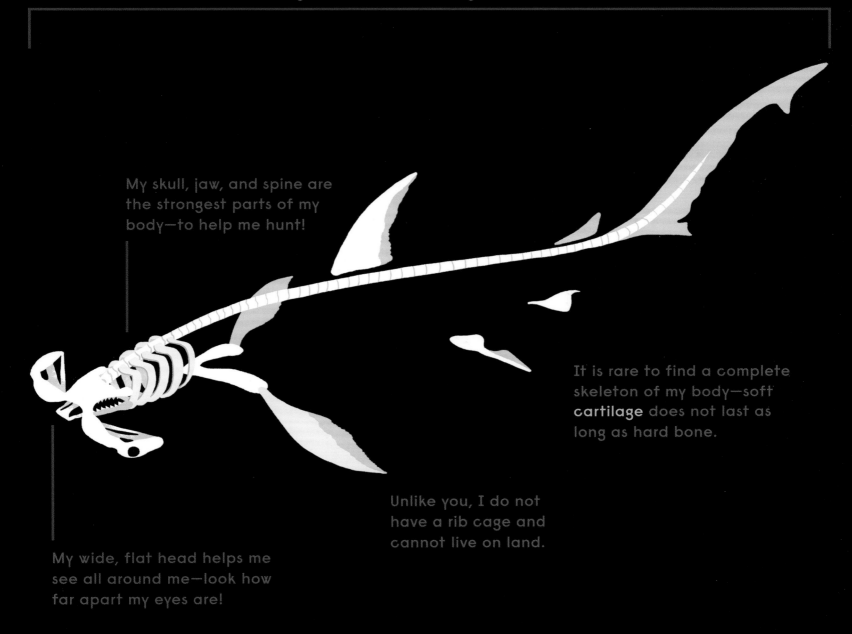

It is rare to find a complete skeleton of my body—soft **cartilage** does not last as long as hard bone.

Unlike you, I do not have a rib cage and cannot live on land.

My wide, flat head helps me see all around me—look how far apart my eyes are!

Who am I?

I AM A GREAT HAMMERHEAD SHARK

Everyone. Wants. To. Talk. About. My. Head. My skull is shaped like a shovel, but I don't use it for digging! It's my best hunting tool. That's right: I use my wide skull to ram and pin a stingray before taking a big gulp and swallowing it whole. You know what also helps me find and TRAP prey? My soft and bendable skeleton. My skeleton is much lighter than one made of bones, so I save a lot of energy when I swim. This makes me an excellent, efficient hunter. There are ten different types of hammerhead sharks. I am the largest.

GUESS WHO ELSE HAS

SPECIAL BONES

YOU do! Like a giraffe, you have seven vertebrae in your neck. Like a bat, you have two hands, each with four fingers and a thumb. Like a snake, you have a bendy and flexible spine. Like a shrew, the smallest bones in your body are the hammer, anvil, and stirrup bones in your ears. Like a moose, your bones grow faster when you eat healthy food. The hardest bone in your body—your mandible—lets you chomp on a nut. Your hand—the body part with the most bones—has 27 bones, and this helps you pick up a grape and play the guitar. Your bones help you eat breakfast, hear a bird chirp, and play basketball.

I like these bones, don't you?

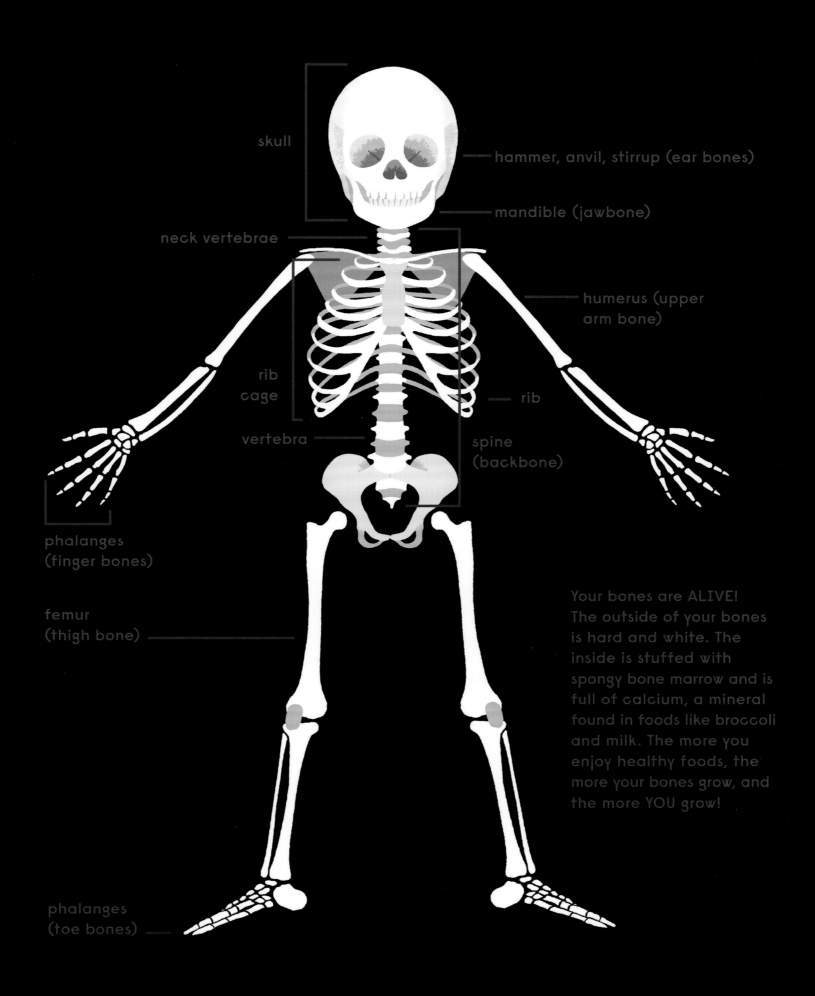

skull

hammer, anvil, stirrup (ear bones)

mandible (jawbone)

neck vertebrae

humerus (upper arm bone)

rib cage

rib

vertebra

spine (backbone)

phalanges (finger bones)

femur (thigh bone)

Your bones are ALIVE! The outside of your bones is hard and white. The inside is stuffed with spongy bone marrow and is full of calcium, a mineral found in foods like broccoli and milk. The more you enjoy healthy foods, the more your bones grow, and the more YOU grow!

phalanges (toe bones)

Dear Reader,

I love reading about animal bones!

The first thing I learned while researching this book is that there is a lot about animal bones that scientists don't yet know. For instance, no one has weighed the bones of *every* bird, or timed how quickly the antlers of a moose grow compared to those of a porcupine caribou.

Why is that? Well, animals are tricky to study! For instance, small and shy animals like the Etruscan shrew can be difficult to track down. And you can hardly invite an enormous blue whale into your classroom! When you do come across an animal, it is difficult to learn about its inside...without taking apart the outside. We want to let an animal live its full life.

48

So, we made some creative choices when choosing which animal to explore for each record-breaking fact. Some choices are based on *relative* size (for instance, while a hummingbird weighs less than a peregrine falcon, the falcon's bones are quite light compared to its body size). And even though we don't know whether the antlers of a moose grow quicker than those of an elk, we *do* know that moose have impressive antlers that are worth examining.

Scientists learn more and more about animals and their bones every year. Perhaps you will become a scientist and help uncover even more about animal bones. I hope you will share your discoveries with us when you do!

Happy researching!
Gabe
Brooklyn, New York

FURTHER READING

At the library

Bones: Skeletons and How They Work, by Steve Jenkins. Scholastic Press, 2010.

Skeletons: An Inside Look at Animals, by Jinny Johnson. Reader's Digest Association, 1994.

Jake's Bones by Jack McGowan-Lowe. Ticktock Books, 2014.

Skulls: An Exploration of Alan Dudley's Curious Collection by Simon Winchester. Black Dog & Leventhal Publishers, Inc, 2012.

On the internet

American Museum of Natural History
www.amnh.org

Animal Diversity Web
animaldiversity.org

National Geographic
kids.nationalgeographic.com

Scientific American
www.scientificamerican.com

Smithsonian's National Zoo & Conservation Biology Institute
nationalzoo.si.edu

GLOSSARY OF BONE WORDS

Now that you are a bone expert, use these words to talk like one, too.

ANTLER: A fast-growing, hard bone that grows from the skull of deer and is used for protection. Unlike horns, antlers are shed each fall and grow again the following spring.

BONE: Bones are strong, hard, living tissues that come in many shapes and sizes. They make up the skeleton that gives you and animals their special shape. Bones support and protect the brain, heart, lungs, and other important soft organs on the inside of your body. The outside of a bone is hard and white. The inside is stuffed with spongy bone marrow. Bones are made of calcium and other materials.

BONE MARROW: A thick, spongy kind of living jelly found inside bones. Bone marrow makes the blood cells that carry oxygen around the body.

CALCIUM: This mineral is found in all living creatures and is essential to growing strong bones and teeth. We get calcium from the foods we eat, like beans, nuts, and spinach.

CARTILAGE: This strong, flexible tissue is found throughout the body of all animals. You can feel it in your nose and ears. The skeleton of some fish, like sharks, is made completely of cartilage.

CRANIUM: The bones in the top part of the skull that protect the brain.

HAMMER, ANVIL, STIRRUP: Three tiny bones in your ears and those of all mammals. These bones vibrate to help you hear.

HORN: A hard bone that grows from the skull of animals like the giraffe, goat, and regal horned lizard and is used for protection. Unlike the antlers of a deer, horns are permanent and continue to grow throughout the animal's life.

HUMERUS: This long, strong bone runs from shoulder to elbow in the upper arm of humans, and in the forelimb of animals.

KERATIN: The horns of a rhinoceros and a regal horned lizard are coated in this protective, tough material. It is also found in beaks, claws, feathers, fingernails, and hair.

MANDIBLE: A very hard, strong bone in the lower jaw that helps animals chew and eat.

PHALANGES: The long bones of the finger and toe. Phalanges help an animal grasp and hold things.

RIB: A long, narrow strip of curved bone that attaches to a vertebra in the mid-back. Several ribs make up the rib cage.

RIB CAGE: A bony, basket-like structure in the chest made of ribs and other bones that protects the heart and lungs.

SKELETON: The framework of bones in humans, and animals with a backbone, that protects the soft organs of the body. The shape of an animal's skeleton helps it fly, crawl, or leap in order to stay safe, healthy, and happy in the ocean, mountains, desert, or wherever it may live.

SKULL: A collection of very hard bones that protects the brain. The skull includes bones of the cranium and jaw.

SPINE: Also known as the backbone, the spine is made of many vertebrae. In humans, it runs from the base of the skull along the center of the back, ending in the sit bone.

TOOTH: The hardest material in the body, the tooth attaches to the jaw and is used for eating. Unlike a bone, a tooth cannot heal itself. In some animals, teeth are used as a weapon. In humans, our teeth also help us speak.

VERTEBRAE: Knob-like bones that make up the spine. Humans have five types of vertebrae.